WOMEN, EARTH, AND CREATOR SPIRIT

ELIZABETH A. JOHNSON

1993 Madeleva Lecture
in Spirituality

PAULIST PRESS
New York/Mahwah

Library of Congress Cataloging-in-Publication Data

Johnson, Elizabeth A., 1941-
    Women, earth, and Creator Spirit / Elizabeth A. Johnson.
      p.   cm.— (Madeleva lecture in spirituality ; 1993)
    Includes bibliographical references.
    ISBN 0-8091-3415-2
    1. Human ecology—Religious aspects—Christianity.   2. Nature—
Religious aspects—Christianity. 3. Holy Spirit. 4. Woman (Christian
theology). 5. Ecofeminism—Religious aspects—Christianity.   I. Title.
II. Series.
BT695.5. J64 1993
261.8'362'082—dc20   92-42018
                                                              CIP

Published by Paulist Press
997 Macarthur Blvd.
Mahwah, N.J. 07430

Printed and bound in the United States of America

TABLE OF CONTENTS

Preface 1

1. The Crisis: Ecocide 5

2. A Taproot of the Crisis:
   The Two-Tiered Universe 10

3. Hearkening to Women's Wisdom 23

4. Discerning Kinship with Earth...............................29

5. Remembering Creator Spirit 41

6. Conversion to the Circle of Earth 61

Appendix 69

Notes 72

Elizabeth A. Johnson, CSJ holds a doctorate from Catholic University of America, and is a faculty member of the Theology Department of Fordham University, New York City. She is author of *Consider Jesus: Waves of Renewal in Christology* (NY: Crossroad, 1990); of *SHE WHO IS: The Mystery of God in Feminist Theological Discourse* (NY: Crossroad, 1992); and of over thirty scholarly articles and chapters. A past member of the Board of Directors of the Catholic Theological Society of America, she currently serves on the Board of Editorial Consultants of *Theological Studies* and on the Advisory Committee to the Dogmatics Section of *Concilium*. She lectures widely to church and academic assemblies at home and abroad.

For the next generation, especially Denise and George, Michael and John, Stephen, Deborah, and Brian, Allison, Kristen, and Rachel, Jesse and Joshua, Christopher and Michelle.

PREFACE

At the National Air and Space Museum in Washington, D.C. and at selected museum theaters around this country, a movie entitled "Blue Planet" is currently being shown. Spliced together from film footage taken by astronauts in orbit around planet Earth, this movie entrances viewers with the loveliness of our planet, a small blue and white marble revolving through the black void of space. From above we see the green and brown shapes of the continents, the blue of the vast oceans, the swirling patterns of the clouds, even the lights of cities like jewels in the night. This planet has the look of a live creature, self-contained, full of information, marvelously skilled at handling the sun. Against a background of inspiring music the commentary focuses on the simple theme that this blue planet is our home, our only home in the vast cosmos.

Then as we revel in the beauty, seen from this perspective for the first time in the history of the human race, comes the hook. The camera slowly zooms in from on high to show billowing smoke from a burning rain forest, brown sludge fanning out into the sea from the mouth of a river, a thick cap of gray polluted air over a city, the fuzz of a dust storm blowing away top soil. Earth-based cameras take up the story to show monkeys and parrots racing away from the flames, only to end up with no habitat, no place to live; fish in large numbers washed up dead on a beach; straggling vegetation on a parched earth; people jammed into slums and shanty towns; children haggard with hunger. The commentary remains the same: this blue planet is our home, our only home in the vast cosmos. But, one is left to conclude, we are wrecking it.[1]

For anyone who believes in a God who creates and sustains the world and who even pronounces it "very good" (Gen 1:31), wasting the world is an ethical, religious, and theological issue of critical importance. Hence Christian theology today is examining its conscience to see where it has traditionally had complicity in the exploitation of the earth, and what resources it can bring to nurture a more wholesome relationship. In this lecture I hope to contribute to this conversation, and to encourage others in the Christian community to bring their own wisdom to bear on this issue.

To be precise: I propose to explore the thesis that the exploitation of the earth, which has reached crisis proportions in our day, is intimately linked to the marginalization of women, and that both of these predicaments are intrinsically related to forgetting the Creator Spirit who pervades the world in the dance of life. Within a sexist system the true identity of both women and the earth are skewed. Both are commonly excluded from the sphere of the sacred; both are routinely taken for granted and ignored, used and discarded, even battered and "raped," while nevertheless they do not cease to give birth and sustain life. Both women and the earth, furthermore, have a symbolic and literal affinity with the Creator Spirit, giver of life, who is similarly ignored in western religious consciousness as a result of restricting the sacred to a transcendent, monarchical deity outside of nature.

These three relationships—human beings to the earth, among each other, and to God—are profoundly interconnected. The way one is cast affects the other two. In the heritage of western thought, of which theology is a part, all three have been conceived primarily according to the values of patriarchy. Thus, for a flourishing human community on a thriving earth to come about, all three must be rethought together in a new vision of wholeness that begins with lifting up what has been disparaged. Technically this lecture is concerned with Christian anthropology, the doctrine of creation, and the doctrine of God. But it approaches these areas of theology from the precise angle of what has been trivialized: women, earth, and Spirit. We seek critical and productive insights that may emerge from the nexus of these disvalued realities to move us in a life-centered direction and away from actions that bequeath desolation to coming generations.

I will treat this issue in three major stages. After a clear look at the present ecological situation, I analyze one of the taproots of the crisis, namely, the rationality of hierarchical dualism. I then turn to three neglected sources of wisdom that contain building blocks of an alternative vision. Here I listen to women's wisdom, discern human connectedness to the earth, and remember the Creator Spirit. Finally, bringing these three together, I argue that our intelli-

3

gence and our hearts need to be converted to the circle of the earth. In my judgment this is not just one more concern among other worthy causes but the most basic one of all. If there be no more living earth, what else is possible? This is a question charged with ethical and religious significance for ourselves and future generations.

1.
THE CRISIS: ECOCIDE

Let us begin by taking a cold, clear-eyed look at the earth's situation today. "Blue Planet" depicts in vivid images what news headlines daily report and what the Earth Summit in Rio de Janeiro in 1992 made clear: unfolding around us is an ecological disaster of ruinous proportions. It seems to be happening in slow-motion, as we count the days. But speeding up the camera of time even a little reveals how rapidly the situation is deteriorating. Naming some of the many crisis points moves language into cadences of biblical, prophetic lament:

• We are poisoning our life-support systems of soil, water, and air with toxic waste such as fumes, chemicals, sewage, detergents, pesticides, and radioactivity. Many pollutants that have already risen into the atmosphere or seeped into the ground cannot be recaptured. We are making the planet unfit for life.

• Through burning, logging, or industrial showers of acid rain we are destroying the earth's forests, ruining the trees that create and purify the air we breathe.

• Largely through the chemicals used in refrigerators, air conditioners, and several industrial processes that serve the life-styles of rich nations, we have torn a hole in the protective ozone layer that shields life on earth from the ultraviolet rays of the sun. In the early millennia of our planet before there was such an ozone envelope, the first living creatures that evolved in the sea had to remain two to three feet below the surface of the water to avoid being frizzled by these rays. It was only after millions of years of these blue-green algae doing their marvelous photo-synthesis act that gives off oxygen as a waste product, and only after millions of years of this oxygen collecting and forming into an ozone layer, that it was safe for life to come out of the depths of the water. And now our generation has ripped an opening in this shield, exposing life to a destructive onslaught of sun-rays.

• Our great oceans are littered with plastic and laced with sewage; many prize fish and mammals are being hunted or harvested to extinction; and the wetlands that provide their spawning ground are being drained or overbuilt.

• We are turning fertile soil into deserts through insensitive agricultural methods, losing roughly eighteen billion tons of topsoil every year. The world is running out of usable farmland; starvation looms.

• Through unlimited human reproduction we are increasing the numbers of our own species exponentially. From the beginning of the human race to the turn of the first Christian millennium (1000 A.D.), human population grew to approximately one-quarter billion people. By 2000 A.D. the number will be six and a quarter billion people; by 2050 A.D., eleven billion. This human population explosion is fast exceeding earth's carrying capacity. It puts increasing pressure on resources and habitat to the point where these become exhausted, causing intense misery to human beings and other creatures alike.

• We are annihilating our companion creatures at a rapid rate. Thousands of species are already extinct, and by a conservative estimate 10,000 species a year continue to be destroyed. We are experiencing in a single lifetime the loss of more than half the living species created by God. Life forms that have taken millions of years to evolve, magnificent animals and intricate plants, disappear forever. Each one, as Meister Eckhart put it, is a word of God, a book about God.[2] Each is important for the life of this planet. We can never bring them back. And they will not evolve this way again.

• The great net of nuclear terror is thrown all over the world, threatening a radioactive conflagration that would effectively annihilate life now and in the foreseeable future.

To say that we are dealing with an environmental "problem" is an understatement. In her essay entitled "Women Against Wasting the World," Catherine Keller consults Webster's Dictionary and finds that to waste something means to ravage it, to devastate it with great violence, as in "to lay waste."[3] At the present moment the earth is still a community of living creatures endowed with powerful, responsive forces for life. But it is being wasted, with great violence, by multiple acts that add up to nothing less than ecocide. Our blue planet as a habitat for life stands in jeopardy due to atmospheric damage, deforestation, pollution of the seas, disruption of ecosystems, destruction of habitat, extinction of species, loss of biodiversity, overpopulation, resource exhaustion, and nuclear proliferation. Lasting damage has already been inflicted, and time is short, since the deterioration of some life-support systems appears to be accelerating. Unless there is a radical reversal soon, we must ask the question whether life, our own and that of future human generations as well as that of myriad living creatures, will flourish on this planet or will pathetically diminish, even disappear.[4]

In the light of this painful reality, people around the world today are thinking new thoughts about the environment. The realization is dawning that for the sake of survival, our own and others, women and men together must be against wasting the world. This awareness, furthermore, is charged with spiritual value as people rediscover the sacred dimension of the earth and the resulting ethical imperative to cherish it.

In the Christian community biblical scholars and theologians are beginning to explicate creation, prophetic wisdom, and gospel traditions in the effort to construct a life-saving environmental ethic and spirituality. The living memory of the gospels, for example, depict Jesus preaching a non-violent ethic pervaded with compassion and mutual regard. He himself lives in tune with the natural world, knowing about growing seeds and harvests, clouds and sunsets, fig trees and weeds, sheep and mother hens. His disciples are instructed to learn lessons about their relationship to God from the birds of the air and the lilies of the field (Mt 6:25-33). His own exuberant desire to feed people and his creative use of bread and wine left communion in these earthly things as the living symbol of his presence to this very day. Indeed, in the light of the resurrection of the one who was crucified on the cosmic tree, the Johannine and later Pauline traditions see that the whole world is created through Christ (Jn 1:3) and is the cosmic body of Christ (Col 1:15-20).

Much excellent work has already been done.[5] Yet to this day and in most quarters the churches, institutionally and in their members, remain curiously unmoved by this most serious moral and religious challenge facing our generation. To use a religious analogy, earth is entering into its passion and death, with newly victimized species and life-systems crying out from the depths, while too many of her disciples seem to think they can avoid what is going on by hiding in some isolated upper room.

2.
A TAPROOT OF THE CRISIS:
THE TWO-TIERED UNIVERSE

I am persuaded of the truth of ecofeminism's insight that analysis of the ecological crisis does not get to the heart of the matter until it sees the connection between exploitation of the earth and the sexist definition and treatment of women.[6] As a theologian I am further convinced that the distortion found in those two instances also influences the Christian experience and doctrine of the mystery of God. This, I suggest, is the genius of women's spirituality in our day, informed by feminist analysis: that it sees the deficient pattern as a whole rather than in bits and pieces. Having faced something of the devastating result, let us cut to a major taproot of the crisis, namely, the dominant form of western rationality called hierarchical dualism.

This is a pattern of thought and action that (1) divides reality into two separate and opposing spheres, and (2) assigns a higher value to one of them. In terms of the three basic relations that shape an ecological ethic, this results in a view in which humanity is detached from and more important than nature; man is separate from and more valuable than woman; God is disconnected from the world, utterly and simply transcendent over it, as well as more significant than it. Hierarchical dualism delivers a two-tiered vision of reality that privileges the elite half of a pair and subordinates the other, which is thought to have little or no intrinsic value of its own but exists only to be of use to the higher.

In the form in which it affects Christian theology and most of western thought, hierarchical dualism was first articulated in ancient Greek philosophy. Here it is envisioned that reality is composed of two separate levels of existence, namely, spirit and matter. Spirit is a transcendent principle that brings into play activity, autonomy, reason, the mind, the intellectual, the soul, the permanent, the infinite. Matter, on the other hand, is the principle signifying immanence which shows itself in passivity, dependence, emotions, the body, the physical, nature, the transitory, the finite.

In some ancient conceptual frameworks matter and spirit thus distinguished exist in a harmonious tension of opposites. But the thought pattern that became most influential in subsequent tradition separated and graded them. Consequently, rather than existing in dialectical interplay, these two spheres of existence are described as polar opposites and their differences are maximized. With a logic that assumes differences automatically signal the presence of something inferior, spirit and matter are also ranked. Spirit is valued more highly than matter, which, as a lower, entrapping element, is meant to be controlled for the sake of spirit. These two aspects of reality, in other words, are separate and unequal.

11

The resulting dichotomy is familiar to anyone educated in western anthropology. The essential self is the soul, which is divided from the body. In the resulting hierarchy of the self, the body is less valued and is even given a negative connotation, while the mind is prized as more permanent, closer to the sphere of divinity, and meant to rule over the recalcitrant flesh.

WOMEN AND EARTH

Feminist reflection brings to the fore another basic element in this construction, namely, that it equates spirit with the masculine principle in the world while matter is identified with the feminine. In terms of actual people, this means that men are linked with a transcendent, spiritual principle beyond nature, while women and the earth embody the lower, material principle, existing with a natural inferiority for which there is no remedy. The hierarchy of mind over body in the individual is therefore not a neutral construction but has political consequences. It translates into social structures of domination/subordination undergirded by the belief that man should rule over woman, the quintessential "Other" whose reproductive power and survival skills he needs and gets but whom he is also free to disparage. This arrangement does not benefit all men, but only those of the ruling classes. Onto other men of the lower classes and different races are also projected the same so-called "feminine" qualities of bodiliness, irrationality, and so forth that cry out for "stronger" male con-

12

trol. "According to Aristotle's *Politics*, ruling class Greek males are the natural exemplars of mind or reason, while women, slaves and barbarians are the naturally servile people who must be subdued and ruled by their 'head'."[7]

This social dualism in the human community, thought to be naturally in tune with the shape of the universe, also has ecological consequences. For the earth is matter, the antithesis of spirit. The ruling man's hierarchy over women and slaves extends also to nature, most often symbolized as female. She is meant for his service while he, in his nobility, has a duty and right to tame and control her. The female symbolism for nature that generally pervades human thought arises from the fact that women are the life-givers to every human child, as the earth itself, Mother Earth, brings forth fruits. Within a system of dualism, however, both women and the natural world are separated from the men they bring forth and sustain. Both are assigned instrumental value, with little or no intrinsic worth apart from their potential to serve the needs and desires of men. Women whose bodies mediate physical existence to humanity thus become symbolically the oldest archetype of the connection between social domination and the domination of nature.

The ancient tree of hierarchical dualism received a new layer of foliage with the advent of the modern age. Philosophers of the Enlightenment era argue in a new way that the mind as knower is separated from all other things that are the object of knowledge. The rational mind (*res cogitans*) is the essential self, while matter, nature, the universe (*res extensa*) stand over against this mind as objects to be explored and mastered. The self, in this view, is essentially solitary and disembodied, the body being an alien material clothing that insulates the discrete psychic substance that is the rational mind. René Descartes' famous axiom, *Cogito, ergo sum,* "I think, therefore I am," sums up this new dualism of body and mind.

Coherent with this view of the body, the emerging Enlightenment philosophy of science quantified nature as a thing. Rather than being the mysterious source and matrix of life, an organism in its own right, nature is now newly envisioned as a machine. It is made up of components that man's rational mind can identify, take apart, and put to work in new ways. Because it is mere matter, lifeless and dead, nature can rightly be probed, subjugated, manipulated. It has, in this view, only instrumental value, of worth only to the degree that man can master it to advance progress. Isaac Newton's image of the world as a gigantic clockwork mechanism, wound up in the beginning by God the watchmaker and now mechanically ticking away by its own inexorable laws, is a memorable depiction of this view.[8]

Hierarchical dualism in both its traditional and modern forms places the privileged, so-called rational man apart from and above other persons such as women, the poor, and people of color, as well as nature, and even his own body. Feminist analysis insists that the devastating ecological consequences of this two-tiered vision cannot be fully addressed until we face it as a whole. We need to understand that an anti-body philosophy is profoundly misogynist. We

14

need to realize that the natural environment is oppressed, manipulated, and abused in ways analogous to the patriarchal use of women. Under patriarchy women are identified literally and symbolically with the natural world. Mutually associated and mutually devalued, both are subjugated in the same act. Their exploitation has a common ideological root: men's separation from and supposed superiority to material femaleness.

In her groundbreaking study *The Death of Nature*, Carolyn Merchant illustrates this in telling detail. The birth of modern science depends on the move to make nature not a great teacher but man's servant, and man not nature's child but her master, in accord with patriarchal rule. Francis Bacon, a celebrated founder of modern scientific method, is one who makes the connection with women's subordination explicit. He speaks of wresting new knowledge from nature's womb; of seizing her by the hair of her head and molding her into something new by technology; of penetrating her mysteries; of having the power to conquer and subdue her. He suggests that nature is a devious female similar to those women in his society who were thought to be witches. He likens the scientific method that interrogates nature to those of the juridical inquisition that examines these women, including torture with mechanical devices as a symbolic tool for wresting from nature her secrets. He writes: "Neither ought a man to make scruple of entering and penetrating into these holes and corners, when the inquisition of truth is his whole object...."[9] His attitude, widely influential for subsequent scientific history, is summed up in his work *The*

Masculine Birth of Time: "I am come in very truth leading to you nature with all her children to bind her to your service and make her your slave."[10]

In our day the mentality that sees nature as something to be dominated more often than not continues to draw on the imagery and attitudes of men's domination of women. For example, the much used phrase "the rape of the earth" reveals the extent to which exploitation of nature is identified with violent sexual conquest of women. Our language speaks of "virgin forest," as yet untouched by man but awaiting his exploration and conquest. Symbolized as female, earth can be made to yield up her secrets; she can be penetrated, conquered, possessed. She is given to man for mastering and as a resource for his pleasure and need. At the same time, to be truly himself man must transcend nature in the pursuit of culture, inevitably described as a masculine endeavor.[11]

These and other linguistic metaphors point to the fact that the social domination of women and the ecological domination of the earth are inextricably fused in theory and practice. Hence the common statement that at the root of our ecological crisis is an overly anthropocentric view of the world is not quite accurate. It would be more precise to say that the problem lies in an androcentric view. Historically, not the superior identity of humanity in general but of man, understood as ruling class males in a patriarchal system, mandates the domination of nature.

Catherine Keller has noted that dualism always comes with the heroic self "who divides so he can conquer."[12] Thus some analysts argue that a primary motivation for the creation of this system is man's

16

profound anxiety about finitude and death. Dualism allows a man to split off the dark side from his essential self, to take his mortality and dependence and project it upon the body, nature, women, the poor, which he can then attempt to conquer and control. There is some truth to this, I think, although it leaves out of the picture what women do to deal with their own anxiety about death. Understanding the motivation for this dualistic system reveals that fear of finitude is its inner engine.

Sexual dualism and its two-tiered universe is a critical taproot of the ecological crisis. With great clarity Rosemary Ruether, a pioneer in feminist theological attention to the earth, sums up the problem. "It is perhaps not too much to say," she writes, "that the Achilles heel of human civilization, which today has reached global genocidal and ecocidal proportions, resides in this false development of maleness through repression of the female."[13]

WOMEN, EARTH, AND SPIRIT

Hierarchical dualism also shapes the classical Christian doctrine of God, who is depicted as the epitome of the masculine half of the dualistic equation. The all holy Other is uncontaminated by matter, utterly transcendent over the world and unaffected by it. The way in which patriarchal authority commands the obedience of women and other creatures on earth serves as a prime analogy for God's relation to the world. Absolutely omnipotent, "He," for such a concept is always designated by the grammatically mascu-

17

line, is the victorious sovereign whose will is law and whom all are meant to serve. Even when this monarchical model graces the Supreme Being with a benevolent attitude, "He" is still intrinsically remote, ruling the universe while not affected by it in any significant way.

The doctrines of the incarnation of the Word and the indwelling of the Spirit ameliorate the religious impact of this divine concept to some extent, connecting God to the historical, finite world. But as long as dualistic logic holds sway, these beliefs and the intimate religious experiences that they express are not allowed to change the fundamental idea of God as such. God remains essentially separated from and over against the world, which is created to serve "Him."

Consequently, a certain cosmic alienation accompanies the sexism that pervades classic Christian spirituality and theology. As material and therefore feminine, nature, the body, sexuality, and women are of themselves separated from the sphere of the sacred. Man alone bears the fullness of the image of God, while women only deficiently so, and nature not at all. Persons seeking spiritual perfection need to extricate themselves from these instances of carnal matter by ascetic practices. The path to holiness is marked "Flee the world." To be holy one must escape the prison of the flesh and its transitory desires and seek a higher world where passion and finitude are overcome. The trivialization of nature is the background against which Christian life, from the spirituality of the individual to the social life of the institution, is shaped by the dualistic legacy of soul over body, man over woman, and God over the world. In every case, it is the dualistically conceived masculine principle *über alles*.

The influence of this massive heritage sheds some light on the peculiar neglect of God the Holy Spirit in western Christianity. The whole church remembers the Spirit on the feast of Pentecost and on the occasion of the sacrament of confirmation; charismatic Christians pray and heal in the power of the Spirit; and local communities may invoke the Spirit before making important decisions, singing the ninth century hymn "Veni Creator Spiritus," "Come, Creator Spirit." But apart from these instances there is little sustained appreciation of the Spirit in an existential or intellectual way. As Heribert Mühlen observes, when most of us say God, the Holy Spirit never comes immediately to mind; rather, the Spirit seems like an edifying appendage to the doctrine of God.[14] In unusually colorful language, theologians today describe the Spirit as the forgotten God, something faceless, shadowy, ghostly, vague, the poor relation in the Trinity, the unknown or half-known God, even the Cinderella of theology.[15]

The logic of hierarchical dualism sheds light on why this is the case. Valuing spirit over body and transcendence over immanence, it concentrates on the one high God who creates by "His" word to the neglect of the indwelling, sustaining presence of God within the fragility of matter and historical process. When this pattern of thought turns to Trinitarian theology it keeps the focus on the relation of Father and Son, one generating and the other being generated, finding it difficult even to know what proper name to

19

give the Spirit. Dualism has trouble with threes.

But it is not only the framework on which the doctrine of God is built that excludes the Spirit. In a subtle way this mindset connects the Spirit with the female side of the dualistic equation, with women's reality and functions, which it disvalues. The Spirit brings forth and nurtures life, keeps all things connected, and constantly renews what the ravages of time and sin break down. This is surely analogous to traditional "women's work" which goes on continuously in home and society, bringing forth life, holding all things together, cleaning what has been messed up, while unnoticed and unremunerated. Neglect of the Spirit has a symbolic affinity with the marginalization of women and is an inevitable outcome of a sexist, dualistic lens on reality, which also, let us remember, disvalues nature.

The extent of what is lost to the richness of faith can be glimpsed when we realize that what is being neglected is nothing less than the mystery of God's personal engagement with the world in its history of love and disaster; nothing less than God's empowering presence active within the cosmos from the beginning, throughout history and to the end, calling forth life and freedom. Forgetting the Spirit is not ignoring a faceless, shadowy, third hypostasis but the mystery of God vivifying the world, closer to us than we are to ourselves, drawing near and passing by in liberating compassion.

Three basic relationships: human beings with nature, among themselves, and with God. In each instance the major classical pattern of relationship is shaped by hierarchical dualism, that is, modeled on

the dominance of ruling male elites and the subjuga-
tion of what is identified as female, cosmic, or for-
eign, an underclass with only instrumental value. As
the ecological crisis makes crystal clear, the polariza-
tion of each pair's terms is nothing short of disastrous
in its interconnected effects. Our eyes have been
blinded to the sacredness of the earth, which is linked
to the exclusion of women from the sphere of the
sacred, which is tied to focus on a monarchical, patriarchal idea of God and a consequent forgetting of the
Creator Spirit, the Lifegiver who is intimately related
to the earth.

In the quest for an ecological ethic grounded in
religious truth, these three relationships need to be
rethought together. But we must be wary of roads
that lead to dead-ends. I think it is a strategic mistake
to retain the dualistic way of thinking and hope to
make an advance simply by assigning greater value to
the repressed "feminine" side of the polarity. This is
to keep women, earth, and Spirit in their pre-assigned
box, which is a cramped, subordinate place. Even if
what has previously been disparaged is now highly
appreciated, this strategy does not allow for the
fullest flourishing of what is confined to one pole by
pre-assigned definition. In truth, women are not any
closer to nature than men are; this is a cultural construct. In truth, women are every bit as rational as
men, every bit as courageous, every bit as capable of
initiative. At the same time, precisely because women
have been so identified with nature, our voices at this
moment in time can speak out for the value of
despised matter, bodies, and nature even as we assert
that women's rational and spiritual capacities are

equal to those of men. What we search for is a way to undercut the dualism and to construct a new, wholistic design for all of reality built on appreciation of difference in a genuine community. We seek a unifying vision that does not stratify what is distinct into superior-inferior layers but reconciles them in relationships of mutuality. Let us then listen to women's wisdom, discern our kinship with the earth, and remember the Spirit, as vital steps toward an ecological ethic and spirituality.

3.
HEARKENING
TO WOMEN'S WISDOM

The wisdom arising from women's experiences today is articulated in theory called feminist, from the Latin *femina*, woman. Christian feminist theology, a branch of this worldwide movement, concerns itself with religious matters in the Christian tradition. It engages in the age-old quest of "faith seeking understanding" in the light of the fundamental principle that, as Margaret Farley articulates it, "women are fully human and are to be valued as such,"[16] a principle not often honored in the theological tradition. Accordingly, feminist theology attends to women for clues as to how they experience and interpret reality, especially spiritual reality, and uses these indicators as guides to construct a vision of a religious and moral universe wherein women's well-being along with everything they treasure is promoted. Christian feminist theology does this in conversation with its own community's founding texts and subsequent tradition. At its heart is the collective imagination of the reign of God that Jesus preached and that the Spirit brings forth: a new world and a new way of being in the world that holds a blessing for all life—women,

men, and their children, all races, the poor, and the earth included. To cooperate in the coming of God's reign, feminist theology argues, the Christian community needs to be transformed into a community of the discipleship of equals as a sacramental witness to the vocation of the whole world. In the face of the centuries-long subordination of women and their concerns, therefore, feminist theology advocates women's flourishing in all their dimensions and relationships as an essential element, missing to date, of the redeemed human community.

Focused by the lens of women's flourishing, feminist theology raises a strong critique against sexism, which is a pattern of thinking and acting that subordinates women on the basis of their sex. In structural terms sexism shows itself as patriarchy, the social arrangement where power is exercised of necessity by the dominant male or males, with others ranked in descending orders of dominance. This results in a social group modeled in the form of a pyramid. In intellectual terms sexism is expressed in androcentrism, the thought pattern that takes the human characteristics of the adult male as normative for the whole of humanity, consigning whatever deviates from this to the outer realms of otherness or deficiency. As both a social arrangement and an ideology, sexism succeeds in making women mostly invisible, inaudible, and marginal, except for the supportive services they provide. "To be in the margin," as Bell Hooks writes, "is to be part of the whole but outside the main body."[17] It is not an unnecessary place, but a place of systematic devaluing. Being there signifies being less, being overlooked, not having as much importance.

24

Running counter to this disparagement, Christian feminist thinking seeks a new wholeness, a new community of the mutuality of equals. It does so in the context of myriad sufferings resulting from women's being demeaned in theory and practice in contradiction to the creative power, dignity and goodness that women appreciate to be intrinsic to their own human identity. Feminist theology results when women's faith seeks understanding in the matrix of historical struggle for life in the face of oppressive and alienating forces.

Its most distinctive move is to consult women's experience both as a reality check for all religious statements and practices, recognizing truth in those that promote women's flourishing and untruth in those that diminish it, and as a neglected source of wisdom about the world that can generate insights much needed today. One of the clearest insights emerging to date is that women tend to experience themselves as a self in fundamental embodied connection with others.[18] I prescind here from the debate over whether this is the result of nature or nurture or both, being loath to stereotype any characteristic as intrinsically masculine or feminine. The point is simply that, given the specific ways they have historically lived in the world, women as a group at this moment of time articulate their self-understanding with a strong accent on relationality.

Classic theology assumes that the self is best defined over against the other. Students of personality formation now point out that this idea reflects primarily a male experience, springing from the pattern of the young boy with his mother.[19] To become himself a boy needs to differentiate himself from his mother. He finds his identity by some measure of separation or opposition to her. When carried unnuanced into adulthood this stance leads to the ideal of the solitary self, the "Cogito, ergo sum" model of self-identity that sees strength in being a sealed, watertight self and that defines power in adversarial relations over against others. The classic idea of God is deeply rooted in this dualistic experience. It conceives of holy mystery on the model of the male self typically constructed over against others. Consequently, the being of God stands over against the world, solitary, superior, untouched by contingency and its pain, and able to best all comers.

The experience of the young girl with her mother yields an alternative paradigm. To become herself the girl does not need to become totally different from her mother. Rather, she matures by a dialectic of identification and differentiation, being and growing with the other in mutually enhancing relation. As a result, adult women establish their identity not in total separation but in a form of relational autonomy, a becoming distinct through interconnection. From this experience feminist theory draws a wisdom which it recommends to all, women and men alike, as a human ideal, namely, the self is rightly structured not in isolation from or dualistic opposition to the other but in intrinsic relationship with the other. Rather than "we" meaning "not they," we and they are intertwined. Neither heteronomy (exclusive other-directedness) nor autonomy in a closed egocentric sense but relational independence, freedom in relation, full related selfhood becomes the ideal. The vision is one of autonomy which honors the inviolable personal mystery of the person who is constituted essentially by relationship with the other.

Not just any pattern of relationship will do, however. A relation structured according to the dominant-subordinate motif inevitably shortchanges the full potential for flourishing of everyone caught in its pyramid. By contrast, women's experience bears out again and again that the most life-giving exchange occurs when bonds are reciprocal or mutual. Mutuality is a form of relation marked by equivalence between persons. It involves a concomitant valuing of each other, a give and take according to each one's strengths and weaknesses, and a common regard marked by trust, affection, and respect for differences—all this in contrast to competition, domination, or assertions of superiority. It is a relationship patterned like friendship, an experience often used to characterize the freedom-connection dialectic at the heart of all mature caring.

Feminist thinking prizes dialectical connectedness that flourishes in a circle of mutuality. This has obvious implications for the idea of God. If relation is at the heart of the universe, if mutuality is a moral excellence, then the deity of God does not consist in being over against and superior to, but expresses itself in freely drawing near and being connected in mutual relation. This, as we will see, is precisely the way the Creator Spirit is present and active in the world.

In the realm of theory, if the self is not defined by opposition but by the dialectic of friendly, constitutive relation, then it becomes possible to reconcile

27

all manner of previously dichotomous elements: self and other, most basically, and consequently matter and spirit, body and soul, passions and mind, embodiedness and self-transcendence, women and men, humanity and the earth. The intuition of interconnection in women's experience deconstructs the pyramid of hierarchical dualism and constructs in its place a circle of mutual, unfettered interconnectedness. Oppositional, either-or thinking which is essential to the dualistic pattern of reality is transformed by a new paradigm of both-and. This shift reunites classical splits and releases hospitality toward disparaged aspects of reality. Regarding humanity's connection to the earth, women's wisdom suggests that the relation is not one of "over against" and "superior to" but "together with," moving in an interactive circle of mutual kinship.

4.
DISCERNING KINSHIP
WITH EARTH

Our era of planetary destruction brings to the fore the question of how we should conceive of our relation to the earth. At least three positions are possible, corresponding to what I would call the absolute kingship, the stewardship, and the kinship models.

The kingship model is the position I have been criticizing in this lecture. It is based on hierarchical dualism that sees humanity separated from the earth and placed in a position of absolute dominion over all other creatures who are made for us. In this view the creatures of the world are ranked according to their participation in the fullness of spirit, with greater value being assigned to those higher up on the great chain of being. At the lowest level is inorganic matter; next comes vegetative matter, followed by animals, human beings, and non-physical spirits or angels. In the progression from the pebble to the peach to the poodle to the person, with women somewhere between the latter two, the higher order of creatures has the right to use and control the lower. This is the patriarchal pyramid again, resulting in a top-down domination of nature by man.

The stewardship model keeps the structure of hierarchical dualism but calls for human beings to be responsible caretakers or guardians of the earth and all its creatures. Having neither fur nor feathers, human beings need to use the earth creatively for shelter, food, and the basics of survival, developing culture as the medium through which these achievements are passed on. But in so doing, they know that they must care for the earth, even in terms of their own self-interest. In this model humanity is still at the top of the pyramid of being but has a duty to protect and preserve what seems weaker and more vulnerable. This position is clearly an improvement over the absolute ruler model, for it guarantees a modicum of respectful use of the earth. Particularly in the political and legal spheres, its vision is highly beneficial for crafting policy. Yet it misses the crucial aspect of human dependence upon that which we steward. Upon reflection the stewardship model itself finds its deepest foundation in the kinship model that traces an organic connection between human beings and the earth.

If separation is not the ideal but connection is; if dualism is not the ideal but the relational embrace of diversity is; if hierarchy is not the ideal but mutuality is; then the kinship model more closely approximates reality. It sees human beings and the earth with all its creatures intrinsically related as companions in a community of life. Because we are all mutually interconnected, the flourishing or damaging of one ultimately affects all. This kinship attitude does not measure differences on a scale of higher or lower ontological dignity but appreciates them as integral elements in the robust thriving of the whole.

Take, for example, trees. Their process of photosynthesis creates oxygen, the most essential, life-sustaining element in the air we breathe. Without trees there would be no animal or human life on this earth; we would all be asphyxiated. Now, biologically speaking, trees do not need human stewardship. Without human beings they existed very well for millennia. Human beings, however, positively need trees in order to breathe. Who, then, needs whom more? By what standard do human beings say that they are more important than trees? At this point in evolutionary history we form one mutually interdependent community of life. We are all kin.

Recommending this kinship attitude Rosemary Ruether uses the metaphor of dance: "We must start thinking of reality as the connecting links of a dance in which each part is equally vital to the whole, rather than the linear competitive model in which the above prospers by defeating and suppressing what is below."[20] The natural world has given birth to all living things, and sustains us all. It is the matrix of our origin, growth, and fulfillment. Articulated within a religious perspective, the kinship stance knows that we humans are interrelated parts and products of a world that is continually being made and nurtured by the Creator Spirit. Its attitude is one of respect for the earth and all living creatures including ourselves as a manifestation of the Spirit's creative energy; its actions cooperate with the Spirit in helping it flourish. What goes on in this stance is neither a sentimental love of nature nor an ignorance that levels all distinctions between human beings and other forms of life. Rather what is involved is a recognition of the

31

truth: human existence is in fact one with the immensity of all that is. Even as a species we are not separate and isolated, but in all our uniqueness, as Sallie McFague so eloquently writes, "We belong, from the cells of our bodies to the finest creations of our minds, to the intricate, constantly changing cosmos."[21]

Cosmic History

Mutual interrelatedness is inscribed at the heart of all reality. This insight is borne out in an uncanny way by contemporary science, from the macro scale of astrophysics to evolutionary biology to the micro world of quantum theory.

Consider the story of the universe, which originated fifteen billion years ago from a single point. Starhawk describes the elegance of what happened: "Out of the point, the swelling; out of the swelling, the egg; out of the egg, the fire; out of the fire, the stars."[22] The so-called Big Bang is the wellspring that poured out matter and energy in an unimaginable act of creation. This material expanded according to a very precisely calibrated rate, neither too fast nor too slow, in an unfurling that is still going on. Its lumpy unevenness allowed swirling galaxies to form as gravity pulled particles together and their dense friction ignited the stars. The lights went on in the universe.

Roughly five billion years ago some of those giant, aging stars collapsed in spectacular supernova explosions. The enormous heat generated by their death forged some of their simpler atoms into heavier elements such as iron, which flew out with the rest of the debris into the cosmos. Some of this cloud of dust and gas condensed and reignited to become our sun, a second generation star. Some of it coalesced in chunks too small to catch fire, forming the planets of our solar system. At first they were all bare, rocky bodies bombarded by asteroids whose impact released entrapped water, methane, and ammonia. Only earth was at the right distance from the sun to permit released steam to condense and rain down, and over eons the mighty oceans took shape. These seas were like a primeval soup that contained all the building blocks of life. Through a wondrous alchemy abetted by intense ultraviolet sunrays, specific molecules connected and another fire ignited, life, more complex and filled with the future than any star's radiance. The oxygen spun off by the ancient blue-green algae rose to form a protective envelope, the ozone layer, and to fill in its underside with breathable air. In the sea jelly fish, worms, and creatures that lived in shells gradually took shape. Out of the sea came the progenitors of plants, insects, amphibians. On the land spread flowers, birds, giant reptiles, mammals. Life was like an advancing tide, fragile and unlikely but unstoppable.

By 180 million years ago, after four billion years of Earth's development (a number that I cannot conceive), this planet had a fully developed biosphere and would have looked as it does today from outer space. Two million years ago all the flora and fauna that we now know had taken shape. But nowhere over the face of the earth was there yet a wisp of smoke from a campfire. By forty thousand years ago bands of *Homo sapiens* roamed as hunter-gatherers. Their creative intelligence now propels life's development ahead with dizzying rapidity. Ten thousand years ago they lived in rural farm villages; five thousand years ago they formed cities and nations and invented written language; two hundred years ago they devised steam engines, starting the industrial revolution; thirty years ago their numbers began to multiply out of proportion to other living species and to Earth's carrying capacity, and the smoldering ecological crisis blazed into a firestorm. Now the water, air, and soil are being rapidly depleted, and all other living things are finding life more difficult, if not impossible, due to the depredations of us, the latecomers. This state of affairs is entirely new.

A crucial insight emerges from this creation story of cosmic and biological evolution. The kinship model of humankind's relation to the world is not just a poetic, good-hearted way of seeing things but the basic truth. We are connected in a most profound way to the universe, having emerged from it. Events in the galaxies produced the iron that makes our blood red and the calcium that makes our bones and teeth white. These and other heavy elements were cooked in the interior of stars and then dispersed when they died to form a second generation solar system with its planets, on one of which the evolution of life and consciousness followed. In the words of scientist Arthur Peacocke:

> Every atom of iron in our blood would not have been there had it not been produced in some galactic explosion billions of years

34

ago and eventually condensed to form the iron in the crust of the earth from which we have emerged.[23]

Chemically, humanity is all of a piece with the cosmos. The same is true of our genes. Molecular biology shows that the same four bases make up the DNA of almost all living things. The genetic structure of cells in our bodies is remarkably similar to the cells in other creatures, bacteria, grasses, fish, horses, the great gray whales. We have all evolved from common ancestors and are kin in this shared, unbroken genetic history. To put it more poetically, we human beings as physical organisms carry within ourselves "the signature of the supernovas and the geology and life history of the Earth."[24]

Living in the present moment, furthermore, involves us in a continuous exchange of material with the earth and other living creatures. Every time we breathe we take in millions of atoms breathed by the rest of humanity within the last two weeks. In our bodies seven percent of the protein molecules break down each day and have to be rebuilt out of matter from the earth (food) and energy from the sun. Seven percent per day is the statistical measure of our interdependence. In view of the consistent recycling of the human body, the epidermis of our skin can be likened ecologically to a pond surface, not so much a shell or wall as a place of exchange. In a very real sense the world is our body.

Earth with its river of life past, present, and future is a rare gem of fantastic beauty. It is even more wondrous when we realize how fine-tuned were the factors that produced it. If restored to a previous stage, the world would in all likelihood not repeat its evolutionary course up to the present, for at each point a different potential might be actualized. Hundreds of historically contingent factors were and continue to be essential parts of evolution, and even a small change in one of them would result in a different outcome, including ourselves.

The relational character of reality discovered by astrophysics and evolutionary biology is reaffirmed by the study of matter at the atomic and subatomic level. Rather than being an inert substance, matter is composed of atoms that are themselves energy events. Atoms are not inanimate particles moving solidly through space but rather dynamic, undulating structures that often act more like waves than stable things. The subatomic particles that go to make up atoms are even more insubstantial. Whirling and swirling, they move around in an apparent state of random flux. In truth, however, they are participating in an inclusive pattern or field that we cannot pin down. At any given instant they may interact and combine, leaving a discernible trail, but there is no way we can predict the outcome. Organized in patterns and relationships, these merest specks of dancing energy form the basis of the tangible world. Consequently, the idea that matter is a self-contained thing with only external relations to other things is antiquated. Made up of dancing particles that are internally constituted by their relationships, matter itself is profoundly social.[25]

36

The human race along with all living creatures is physically made of the dust of the earth which is the fallout of stardust. But, one might argue, what about intelligence and freedom which so distinguish the human species? Does this not break the kinship that humanity shares with the rest of creation? Not at all. Human consciousness is in continuity with the energy of matter stretching back through galactic ages to the Big Bang, being a special, intense form of this energy. The law of complexity-consciousness reveals that ever more intricate physical combinations, as can be traced in the evolution of the brain, yield ever more powerful forms of spirit. Matter, alive with energy, evolves to spirit. While distinctive, human intelligence and creativity rise out of the very nature of the universe, which is itself intelligent and creative. In other words, human spirit is the cosmos come to consciousness. Teilhard de Chardin broached this point years ago as he wrote, "The human person is the sum total of fifteen billion years of unbroken evolution now thinking about itself."[26] In her search for ecological wisdom Joanna Macy recounts a conversation that yields a similar insight:

> One day, under the vine-strung jungles of eastern Australia, I was walking with my friend John Seed, director of the Rainforest Information Centre. I asked him how he managed to overcome despair and sustain the struggle against the mammoth timber interests. He said, "I try to

remember it's not me, John Seed, trying to protect the rainforest. Rather I am part of the rainforest protecting myself. I am that part of the rainforest recently emerged into human thinking."[27]

Human spirit expressed in self-consciousness and freedom is not something new added to the universe from outside. Rather, it is a sophisticated evolutionary expression of the capacity for self-organization and creativity inherent in the universe itself. In Thomas Berry's metaphor, we are part of a great journey, the journey of primordial matter through its marvelous sequence of transformations in the stars, in the earth, in living creatures, in human consciousness. This makes us distinct but not separate, a unique strand in the cosmos, yet still a strand *of* the cosmos. Consciousness is the flowering through us of deeply cosmic energies. Thus human spirit is rightly interpreted *within* rather than *over against* human kinship with nature.

Since nature is a dynamic web of interconnected processes of which we are one part, it becomes clear that each species that has evolved has an intrinsic value of its own, apart from immediate human use. The kinship paradigm appreciates this even as it knows our own human difference. For it arises from an experience of communion which at its deepest level is religious. From a religious perspective, all diverse strands in the web of life are expressions of the creative power of the cosmos which is ultimately empowered by the Creator Spirit. The enormous diversity of species itself points to the inexhaustible

38

richness of the Creator, whose imaginative goodness these species represent. As Aquinas ruminates:

> For he [i.e. God] brought things into being in order that his goodness might be communicated to creatures, and be represented through them. And because his goodness could not be adequately represented by one creature alone, he produced many and diverse creatures, that what was wanting to one in the representation of divine goodness might be supplied by another. For goodness, which in God is simple and uniform, in creatures is manifold and divided. Hence the universe as a whole participates in and represents divine goodness more perfectly than any single creature alone.[28]

Realizing this, the religious kinship attitude cherishes and seeks intelligently to preserve biodiversity, for when a species goes extinct we have lost a manifestation of the goodness of God.

To sum up: appreciating the deep patterns of affiliation in the cosmos, the kinship model knows that we are all connected. For all our distinctiveness, human beings are modes of being of the universe. Woven into our lives is the very fire from the stars and the genes from the sea creatures, and everyone, utterly everyone, is kin in the radiant tapestry of being. This relationship is not external or extrinsic to who we are, but wells up as the defining truth from our deepest being. "Humans and yeast are kin," writes physicist Brian Swimme of this cosmic fact:

> They organize themselves chemically and
> biologically in nearly indistinguishable pat-
> terns of intelligent activity. They speak the
> same genetic language. All things whether
> living or not are descendants of the super-
> nova explosion. All that exists shapes the
> same energy erupting into the universe as
> the primeval fireball. No tribal myth, no
> matter how wild, ever imagined a more
> profound relationship connecting all
> things in an internal way right from the
> beginning. All thinking must begin with
> this cosmic genetical relatedness.[29]

Hearkening to women's wisdom and discerning
kinship with the earth yield the same result, namely, a
transformation of the hierarchical, two-tiered view of
the world into a vision of the community of creation,
necessary if life is to be cherished and preserved. At
the most basic level, however, the ecological crisis
requires us to rethink our idea of God and God's relation to the world in order to direct our action aright
in harmony with divine care. What must the Creator
be like, in whose image this astounding universe is
created? Realization of its energy, diversity, relationality, fecundity, spontaneity, and ever surprising mix-
ture of law and chance makes the times ripe for a
rediscovery of the neglected tradition of the Creator
Spirit.

5.
REMEMBERING CREATOR SPIRIT

GOD WHO ARRIVES

Within a Trinitarian framework the "person" of the Spirit refers primarily to God present and active in the world. Early Christian theology illustrated this by a series of natural metaphors that remain helpful in their illuminating power. If the great, unknowable mystery of God is pictured as the glowing sun, and God incarnate as a ray of that same light streaming to the earth (Christ the sunbeam), then Spirit is the point of light that actually arrives and affects the earth with warmth and energy. And it is all the one light. Again, the transcendent God is like an upwelling spring of water, and a river that flows outward from this source, and the irrigation channel where the water meets and moistens the earth (Spirit). And it is all the one water. Yet again, the triune God is like a plant with its root, shoot, and fruit: deep, invisible root, green stem reaching into the world, and flower that opens to spread beauty and fragrance and to fructify the earth with fruit and seed (Spirit). And it is all the one living plant.[30]

The point for our pondering is that speaking

about the Spirit signifies the presence of the living God active in this historical world. The Spirit is God who actually arrives in every moment, God drawing near and passing by in vivifying power in the midst of historical struggle. So profoundly is this the case that whenever people speak in a generic way of "God," of their experience of God or of God's doing something in the world, more often than not they are referring to the Spirit, if a triune prism be introduced.

Of all the activities that theology attributes to the Spirit, the most significant is this: the Spirit is the creative origin of all life. In the words of the Nicene Creed, the Spirit is *vivificantem,* vivifier or life-giver. This designation refers to creation not just at the beginning of time but continuously: the Spirit is the unceasing, dynamic flow of divine power that sustains the universe, bringing forth life. From this primordial religious intuition, three other insights reverberate.

First, as the continuous creative origin of life the Creator Spirit is immanent in the historical world. "Where can I go from your presence," sings the psalmist, "and from your Spirit where can I flee?" The Spirit is in the highest sky, the deepest hole, the darkest night, farther east than the sunrise, over every next horizon (Ps 139:7-12). The Spirit fills the world and is in all things. Since the Spirit is also transcendent over the world, divine indwelling circles round to embrace the whole world, which thereby dwells within the sphere of the divine. Technically this is known as panentheism, or the existence of all things in God. Distinct from classical theism which separates God and the world, and also different from pantheism which merges God and the world, panentheism

42

holds that the universe, both matter and spirit, is encompassed by the Matrix of the living God in an encircling that generates freedom, self-transcendence, and the future, all in the context of the interconnected whole. The relationship created by this mutual indwelling, while non-hierarchical and reciprocal, is not strictly symmetrical, for the world is dependent on God in a way that God is not on the world. Yet the Spirit's encircling indwelling weaves a genuine solidarity among all creatures and between God and the world.

Second, when things get broken, which can happen so easily, this divine creative power assumes the shape of a rejuvenating energy that renews the face of the earth (Ps 104:30). The damaged earth, violent and unjust social structures, the lonely and broken heart—all cry out for a fresh start. In the midst of this suffering the Creator Spirit, through the mediation of created powers, comes, as the Pentecost sequence sings, to wash what is unclean; to pour water upon what is drought-stricken; to heal what is hurt; to loosen up what is rigid; to warm what is freezing; to straighten out what is crooked and bent.[31] When Jesus reads from the scroll of Isaiah in the Nazareth synagogue, he highlights this point with explicit examples. The Spirit who was upon him had sent him to bring good news to the poor, to proclaim release to captives, sight to the blind, and liberty to the oppressed (Lk 4:16-20). The resurrection of Jesus from the dead into the new life of glory is but the most surprising revelation of this characteristic of the Creator Spirit. Precisely as the giver of life the creative Spirit cherishes what has been made and renews it in myriad ways.

Third, the continuous changing of historical life reveals that the Spirit *moves*. From the beginning of the cosmos, when the Spirit moves over the waters (Gen 1:2), to the end, when God will make all things new (Rev 21:5), standing still is an unknown stance. The long and unfinished development known as evolution testifies to just how much novelty, just how much surprise, the universe is capable of spawning out of pre-given order or chaos. In every instance the living Spirit empowers, lures, prods, dances on ahead. Throughout the process, the Spirit characteristically sets up bonds of kinship among all creatures, human and non-human alike, all of whom are energized by this one Source. A Christian liturgical greeting expresses this very beautifully: "The grace of our Lord Jesus Christ, and the love of God, and the fellowship of the Holy Spirit be with you all." Fellowship, community, *koinonia* is the primordial design of existence, as all creatures are connected through the indwelling, renewing, moving Creator Spirit.

The fundamental insight that the Spirit is the giver of life with its three corollaries of the Spirit's renewing, indwelling, and moving power cry out for concrete, imaginative expression. How shall we speak of Creator Spirit? If we search the scriptures with our major thesis in mind, we find a small collection of cosmic and female symbols of the Spirit, most of which are marginalized by a patriarchal imagination. Remembering these texts can give us the beginnings of a vocabulary for an ecological ethic and spirituality.

44

Among the elements of the natural world that biblical writers deem to have an affinity with the Spirit, the most important are wind, fire, and water.[32] In Hebrew the word for spirit, *ruah*, means moving air or wind. The term encompasses all the movements of wind, from the small, gentle breeze caressing our cheek to the mighty storm gale that reshapes the landscape. The Spirit is like this invisible, natural force, a power that declares itself in the movement of the wind. Jesus spoke of this symbol in a beautifully allusive way: the wind blows where it chooses; you hear the sound of it, but you do not see where it comes from nor where it is going. But you know it is passing by when you see its effects. So it is with the Spirit of God (Jn 3:8).

The Spirit can be likened to the wind and can be discerned as actively present in dramatic, wind-blown events. Think of the strong wind that blows back the Reed Sea so the escaping slaves can run free (Ex 14:21); and of the wind that blows through the valley of the dry bones, breathing life into the vast multitude (Ez 37:1-14); and of the mighty Pentecost wind that shakes the house where Jesus' disciples, women and men alike, are praying, impelling them to public witness of the good news (Acts 1:13-14; 2:1-4). But the blowing Spirit can also be discerned in mundane events, none the less wondrous for being so regular. The warm breezes of spring melt the winter ice, producing flowing waters that green the earth (Ps 147:18).

Wind is connected with wings. The symbol of

the bird and her wings signified female deity in ancient Near East religions. In Greek mythology, as Ann Belford Ulanov points out, the dove is the emblem of Aphrodite, goddess of love. Doves were even cultically protected, with towers erected for them and a steady supply of food provided. The figure of the dove in the gospels and in Christian art thus links the Holy Spirit with the broad pre-Christian tradition of divine female power: "Iconographically the dove is a messenger of the goddess and of the Holy Spirit."[33] Whether hovering like a nesting mother bird over the egg of primordial chaos in the beginning (Gen 1:2); or sheltering those in difficulty under the protective shadow of her wings (Pss 17:8; 36:7; 57:1; 61:4; 91:1,4; Is 31:5); or bearing the enslaved up on her great wings toward freedom (Ex 19:4; Deut 32:11-12); or resting on Jesus to grace and mission him during his baptism (Lk 3:22), the Spirit's activity is evoked with allusion to femaleness.

Ruah, finally, is linked with the breath in the throats of both animals and people. Its presence gives life (Gen 2:7; 7:15); its withdrawal means death (Ps 104:29-30). It makes words, especially prophetic ones (Zech 7:12). Here the primary analogue for Creator Spirit is the distinctive vitality, creativity, and mystery of the human spirit itself.

Drawn by the evocative power of the wind, Meinrad Craighead, artist and religious thinker, muses that "Perhaps it is the wind's infinity which excites that vertiginous desire for edgelessness. It is a longing to be inside the rhythm and duration of the Spirit's inhalation and exhalation, prolonged into the void, east of the sun and west of the moon."[34]

46

Likening this symbol of Creator Spirit to the Native American indwelling spirit named Old Wind Woman, she continues:

> The dark wind of my Mother expands and contracts, winding to and from the hub of the spinning wheel, which is everywhere. She spirals, uncoiling and recoiling, leaving and returning to her source; her spirit evolving, involving the entire universe.[35]

Signifying the Spirit of God with the symbol of wind already begins to transcend the hard dualism of spirit and matter played out in divine unrelatedness to the world. The whole community of creation is sustained by the breath, the Spirit of God, who "rides on the wings of the wind" (Ps 104:3) in profound, if free, connection.

Fire is another cosmic symbol of the Spirit. There is no definite shape to fire, and its ever-changing form signifies something that is unto itself, mysterious. It is a dangerous element that sears if you touch it and that can easily escape human control. At the same time, the light and heat that emanate from fire are indispensable to human well-being. It points to the greater fires in the universe, the glowing sun and stars, and the fierce lightning storms. All are powerful biblical symbols of the presence of God. A bush burns but is not consumed as Moses hears the compassionate message of deliverance from slavery (Ex 3:1-12). Tongues of fire, streams of ardent heat, are seen above the heads of the women and men who will bring the good news of the risen Christ to the whole world (Acts 2:1-3). To borrow the analogy of a fourth century theologian, if fire passing through a mass of iron makes the whole of it glow, so that what was cold becomes burning and what was black is made bright, so too does the power of the Spirit transform hearts and minds, and indeed the clay of creation itself.[36] Perhaps no one has captured the evocative power of this symbol better than Hildegard of Bingen when she writes of the Spirit:

> I, the highest and fiery power, have kin-
> dled every living spark and I have breathed
> out nothing that can die.... I flame above
> the beauty of the fields; I shine in the
> waters; in the sun, the moon and the stars,
> I burn. And by means of the airy wind, I
> stir everything into quickness with a cer-
> tain invisible life which sustains all.... I, the
> fiery power, lie hidden in these things and
> they blaze from me.[37]

Contemporary scientific theory about the origin of the universe in a primeval explosion, inelegantly named the Big Bang, releases yet another layer of meaning from this symbol. The act of creation is already a Pentecost, a first and permanent outpouring of the fiery Spirit of life.

Water is elemental, absolutely essential for life as we know it, although like fire it too can kill. On this planet life began in the primeval seas, and human and other mammalian life continues to originate in the water of the womb. Sap in the tree, dew on the grass, blood in the veins, wine in the vessel, rain on the

48

earth, water outpoured: all bespeak the active presence of God. As a symbol of the Spirit, water points to the bottomless wellspring of the source of life and to the refreshment and gladness that result from deep immersion in this mystery.

Scripture is replete with instances where water symbolizes the Spirit of life. Speaking through the prophet Ezekiel, God promises that the people will find their true heart: "I will sprinkle clean water upon you...and a new spirit I will put within you; and I will remove from your body the heart of stone and give you a heart of flesh" (Ez 36:25-26). In Isaiah's vision, justice and peace in the human world and the natural world are the gifts that result when the Spirit, like a cascade of water from a vessel, is poured out (Is 32:15-18). For Joel, sons and daughters will prophesy and even the old will dream again when drenched with this Spirit poured out on all flesh (Jl 2:28-29). This same Spirit is the living water Jesus promised to the Samaritan woman, a spring of love welling up at the core of creation (Jn 4:7-15). As Paul points out to the Romans, God overflows in the depth of the divine being and from there "the love of God is poured into our hearts by the Holy Spirit given to us" (Rom 5:5).

The poetry of water and the Spirit enticed some early Christian theologians to flights of rhetoric. The second century bishop Irenaeus, for example, describing the life of his community, wrote:

> Just as dry wheat cannot be shaped into a cohesive lump of dough or a loaf held together without moisture, so in the same way we many could not become one...

49

without the water that comes from heaven. As dry earth bears no fruit unless it receives moisture, so we also were originally dry wood and could never have borne the fruit of life without the rain freely given from above.... [we] have received it through the Spirit.[38]

With an eye on the natural world Cyril of Jerusalem observed:

Why did he [Christ] call the grace of the Spirit water? Because by water all things subsist; because water brings forth grass and living things; because the water of the showers comes down from heaven; because it comes down in one form but works in many forms...it becomes white in the lily, red in the rose, purple in violets and hyacinths, different and varied in each species. It is one thing in the palm tree, yet another in the vine, and yet all in all things.[39]

To sum up: the Spirit is life that gives life. She is radiant life energy that like wind, fire, and water awakens and enlivens all things. Each of these symbols has a numinous quality that evokes better than abstract words the presence of the Creator Spirit in the world, moving over the void, breathing into the chaos, pouring out, informing, quickening, warming, setting free, blessing, dancing in mutual immanence with the world.

In the course of her visionary work on Christian doctrine Hildegaard spun out variations on these images that bring home the Spirit's vivifying movement in a lustrous way. The Spirit, she writes, is the life of the life of all creatures; the way in which everything is penetrated with connectedness and relatedness; a burning fire who sparks, ignites, inflames, kindles hearts; a guide in the fog; a balm for wounds; a shining serenity; an overflowing fountain that spreads to all sides. The Spirit is life, movement, color, radiance, restorative stillness in the din. She pours the juice of contrition into hardened hearts. Her power makes dry twigs and withered souls green again with the juice of life. She purifies, absolves, strengthens, heals, gathers the perplexed, seeks the lost. She plays music in the soul, being herself the melody of praise and joy. She awakens mighty hope, blowing everywhere the winds of renewal in creation.[40] Hildegaard's rhetoric puts me in mind of the encouragement offered in the fourth century by Basil of Caesarea in his great work on the Spirit. Let us not be afraid of being too extravagant in what we say about the Holy Spirit, he writes; our thoughts will always fall short.[41]

FEMALE SYMBOLS

It is an interesting point, and one of the saving graces of the religious patriarchal tradition, that in addition to the natural world women's reality is also thought suitable to image the Spirit. The most extended biblical instance of female imagery of the Spirit occurs in the wisdom literature where the

Spirit's functions are depicted as acts of Woman Wisdom. The female figure of Wisdom is the most acutely developed personification of God's presence and activity in the Hebrew scriptures. Not only is the grammatical gender of the word for wisdom feminine *(hokmah* in Hebrew, *sophia* in Greek), but the biblical portrait of Wisdom is consistently female, casting her as sister, mother, female beloved, chef and hostess, teacher, preacher, maker of justice, and a host of other women's roles. In every instance Wisdom symbolizes transcendent power pervading and ordering the world, both nature and human beings, interacting with them all to lure them onto the path of life.[42]

Early in the book of Wisdom this female figure is identified with spirit, a people-loving spirit: "Wisdom is a kindly spirit" (1:6). In a subsequent passage the metaphor shifts slightly to say that Wisdom has a spirit. Her spirit is then described in glorious vocabulary with twenty-one attributes, or three times the perfect number seven. She is:

> intelligent, holy, unique, manifold, subtle, mobile, clear, unpolluted, distinct, invulnerable, loving the good, keen, irresistible, beneficent, humane, steadfast, sure, free from anxiety, all-powerful, overseeing all, and penetrating through all other intelligent spirits (7:22-23).

Poetic parallelism clinches the Wisdom-Spirit equivalence: "Who has learned thy counsel, unless you have given Wisdom, and sent your Holy Spirit from on high?" (Wis 9:17). These and other allusive wisdom texts point to the fittingness of speaking about the Spirit in female imagery, given Sophia's undoubted female symbolization.

Understanding this equivalence, we read the wisdom texts and find magnificent renderings of creation and redemption themes in female symbols. As the Nicene Creed would later say of the Spirit, these texts say of Wisdom that she is the giver of life, she is a tree of life, "she is your life" (Prov 4:13). So intimately is the divine blessing of life associated with her that she can proclaim "whoever finds me finds life" (Prov 8:35). All life is a gift and Woman Wisdom, a personification of the Creator Spirit, gives that gift. She is the "fashioner of all things" (Wis 7:22), responsible for their existence and therefore knowing their inmost secrets. She knows the solstices and changes of the seasons, the constellations of the stars, the natures of animals and the tempers of wild beasts, the variety of plants and the virtues of roots, and the ways of human reasoning (Wis 7:17-22). This passage from the book of Wisdom contains a poignant aside. Solomon, while rejoicing to learn about these things from Wisdom, admits "but I did not know that she was their mother" (Wis 7:12).

It is not just individual creatures who are the subject of Spirit-Sophia's life-giving knowledge, but the world as a whole is shaped harmoniously by her guidance: "She reaches mightily from one end of the earth to the other, and she orders all things well" (Wis 8:1). This ordering is a righteous one, inimical to exploitation and oppression. Sophia hates the ways of arrogance and evil but works to establish just governance on the earth: "By me kings reign, and rulers

53

decree what is just" (Prov 8:15). Indeed, the echoes of the prophetic promise of shalom sound in her self-description: "I walk in the way of righteousness, in the paths of justice" (Prov 8:20).

Spirit-Sophia's presence fills the world: "For Wisdom is more mobile than any motion; because of her pureness she pervades and penetrates all things" (Wis 7:24). This is the same divine presence spoken about in the Jewish rabbinic tradition of the *shekinah*, the female symbol of God's indwelling, the weighty radiance that flashes out in unexpected ways in the midst of the broken world. Most significant is her work of accompaniment, for "Wherever the righteous go, the Shekinah goes with them."[43] No place is too hostile. She accompanies the people through the post-slavery wilderness, and hundreds of years later into exile again, through all the byways of rough times. "Come and see how beloved are the Israelites before God, for withersoever they journeyed in their captivity the Shekinah journeyed with them."[44] In other words, God's indwelling Spirit was with them and this accompaniment gave rise to hope in their suffering.

Virtually every aspect of the Creator Spirit's activity in the world, as delineated in doctrine and theology, is depicted in the wisdom literature in female symbolism. When things become damaged, the power to refresh them pours out from her: "while remaining in herself, she renews all things" (Wis 7:27). This renewing energy profoundly affects human beings in their relation to divine mystery and the rest of the world, weaving them round with a web of kinship: "in every generation she passes into holy souls and makes them friends of God, and prophets"

(Wis 7:27). One aspect of Wisdom has not been seriously appropriated by Christian doctrine of the Spirit, but its time may be coming. The great creation poem of Proverbs shows us creative Wisdom actually playing in the newly minted world, delighting in it all, especially in those intelligent creatures called human (8:22-31).

In addition to the texts about Wisdom, biblical books hold a constellation of maternal images that delineate the Spirit's work in the world. Jesus' conversation with Nicodemus, for example, carries a clear presentation of God the Spirit as mother. A person must be born anew in order to enter the reign of God, Jesus insists, to which Nicodemus queries, "How can anyone be born after having grown old? Can one enter a second time into the mother's womb and be born?" (Jn 3:4). Jesus' reply keeps the metaphor of physical birth and amplifies it to speak of Spirit: "No one can enter the reign of God without being born of water and the Spirit. What is born of the flesh is flesh, and what is born of the Spirit is spirit" (3:5-6). Creator Spirit is here likened to a woman giving birth to offspring who are henceforth truly identified as "born of God."[45]

Other fragments of women's experience of mothering also provide biblical writers symbolic material for Creator Spirit. Like a woman with her knitting needles she knits together the new life in a mother's womb (Ps 139:13); like a woman in childbirth she labors and pants to bring about the birth of justice (Is 42:14); like a midwife she works deftly with a woman in pain to deliver the new creation (Ps 22:9-10); like a washerwoman she scrubs away at bloody stains till the people be like new (Is 4:4; Ps 51:7).

The early Christian centuries carried forward explicit use of female imagery to characterize God's Spirit. In Syriac Christianity, for example, the Spirit's image was consistently that of the brooding or hovering mother bird tending to her chicks. This symbolism of the motherhood of the Spirit fostered a spirituality characterized by warmth which expressed itself in private and public prayer. In one prayer the believer meditates:

> As the wings of doves over their nestlings,
> And the mouths of their nestlings toward their
> mouths,
> So also are the wings of the Spirit over my
> heart.[46]

In another prayer spoken in the context of liturgy the community implores the Spirit:

> The world considers you a merciful mother. Bring with you calm and peace, and spread your wings over our sinful times.[47]

In time most of this maternal imagery migrated away from the Spirit and accrued to the church, called Holy Mother the Church, or to Mary the mother of Jesus, venerated as mother of the faithful as well. The symbol of the maternity of the Spirit was virtually forgotten, along with the capacity of images of Wisdom and Shekinah to evoke divine presence and activity in female form. But this resonance abides in the texts of scripture and tradition, and can be retrieved.

56

Looked at against the background of hierarchical dualism, female and cosmic symbols of the Creator Spirit and the insights to which they give rise have unique potential to heal divided consciousness. The One who blows the wild wind of life, who fires the blaze of being, who gives birth to the world, or who midwifes it into existence does not stand over against it or rule it hierarchically from afar but dwells in intimate, quickening relationship with humanity and the life of the earth. The female symbols in particular dramatize that being women and being fertile is not a dangerous, polluted state but a participation in the fecundity of the Creator Spirit and, conversely, a sign of her presence. Enfolding and unfolding the universe, the Spirit is holy mystery "over all and through all and in all" (Eph 4:6). Remembering Creator Spirit this way dismantles the theological dualism that sets God apart from the universe, thus removing one of the pillars of support for dualism within the human community and between human beings and the earth. We are all woven into the fabric of the one cosmic community. Indeed, God is not far from any one of us, for in her we live and move and have our being, as some of our poets now say (cf. Acts 17:28).

DIVINE RELATION TO THE WORLD

Using cosmic and female images for the Spirit's presence and action in the world enables our minds to attend to the pattern of divine relation to the world in ways that are ecologically helpful. The Spirit

57

is the great, creative Matrix who grounds and sustains the cosmos and attracts it toward the future. Throughout the vast sweep of cosmic and biological evolution she embraces the material root of existence and its endless new potential, empowering the cosmic process from within. The universe, in turn, is self-organizing and self-transcending, corresponding from the spiraling galaxies to the double helix of the DNA molecule to the dance of her quickening power. The Spirit's action does not supplant that of creatures but works cooperatively in and through created action, random, ordered, or free. Nor does the Spirit's dynamic power arrive as an intervention from "outside," but is immanent in the world that is becoming. In keeping with this view, the scientist and religious thinker Arthur Peacocke suggests that a fitting image for the Creator Spirit would be that of a choreographer of an unfinished dance, ingeniously improvising steps for a piece that requires the creativity of the dancers to complete.[48] The relation is not one of dominating or commanding power over, but one of reverent, empowering love.

This does not exclude the enormous amounts of violence, entropy, and suffering that exist throughout the cosmos. Stars are born and die, species appear and disappear due to natural catastrophe, individuals know debilitating pain. We may well wonder how Love could be empowering such a messy and at times tragic arrangement, made more so by the advent of conscious human beings with our historical propensity to sin, to hurt others. I have thought about this all my life, and have read what many wise minds have said, and the bottom line is that nobody knows. What can be ventured is that it has something to do with the nature of love. Love grants autonomy to the beloved and respects this, all the while participating in the joy and pain of the other's destiny. It vigorously cares and works for and urges the beloved toward his or her own well-being, but never forces.

In an open-ended, evolutionary universe death often becomes the matrix for the birth of the new: earth from an exploding star, mushrooms from a rotting tree trunk, a new community from the cross of Jesus. At other times there is no obvious productive outcome, simply the disastrous surd of evil. In either case, the Love who is the Creator Spirit participates in the world's destiny. She can be grieved (Eph 4:30); she can even be quenched (1 Thes 5:19). When creation groans in labor pains and we do too (Rom 8:22-23), the Spirit is in the groaning and in the midwifing that breathes rhythmically along and cooperates in the birth. In other words, in the midst of the agony and delight of the world the Creator Spirit has the character of compassion. In multifaceted relationships she resists, reconciles, accompanies, sympathizes, liberates, comforts, plays, delights, befriends, strengthens, suffers with, vivifies, renews, endures, challenges, participates, all the while moving the world toward its destiny. Moved by this Spirit, human beings are similarly configured to compassion, taught to be co-creators who enter the lists on behalf of those who suffer, to resist and creatively transform the powers that destroy.

A theology of the Creator Spirit overcomes the dualism of spirit and matter with all of its ramifications, and leads to the realization of the sacredness of the earth. The Spirit of God dwelling in the world with quickening power deconstructs dualism and draws in its place a circle of mutuality and inclusiveness. Instead of matter being divorced from spirit and consigned to a realm separate from the holy, it is an intrinsic part of the cosmic community, vivified, indwelt, and renewed by the Creator Spirit. The Spirit creates matter. Matter bears the mark of the sacred and has itself a spiritual radiance. Hence the world is holy, nature is holy, bodies are holy, women's bodies are holy. For the Spirit creates what is physical—worlds, bodies, senses, sexuality, passions—and moves in these every bit as much as in minds and ideas. About the Creator Spirit this can be said: loves bodies, loves to dance. The whole complex, material universe is pervaded and signed by her graceful vigor.

6.
CONVERSION TO THE CIRCLE OF EARTH

This lecture began with the image of a unique blue planet, rapidly being ravaged in our day. We criticized traditional dualistic rationality for complicity in this destruction, seeing the origin of aggression in the failure of connection. Convinced that it would be a mistake to underestimate the role patriarchy plays in shaping the present crisis, we moved on to explore how feminist, scientific, and theological wisdom combine to present an alternative paradigm of the community of creation.

Throughout, I have been reflecting with a sense of urgency. Much of the havoc already wrought is irreversible, and the destructive pace is speeding up in general, despite zones of respite due to good will and good law. If we stay the present course, life will continue to dim on this planet and misery to multiply. Undoing the earth like this is an act of violence against the earth itself, yes, but also against future generations of all species. What, then, are we to do?

There are tough ethical and political decisions to be made, decisions about constraint of consumption, restraint of population growth, development of pollution controls, evolution of industries and trade, and the like. Undergirding all of these is a religious matter. The Creator Spirit's dynamic activity, as we have seen, issues in abundance, diversity, interrelatedness, and manifold possibilities. Human beings violate these patterns by thoughtless or willful harm to the living earth that reduces diversity, breaks up relatedness, and cuts off future possibilities. Hence the damage can begin to be healed only by conversion, meant here in the biblical sense of *metanoia*, a turning around. We must allow ourselves to be converted to the patterns established by the Spirit in the giving of life itself. What is crucial for a viable future is a religious spirit that converts us to the earth.

Our intelligence needs to be converted to the earth, as does our heart, and this involves several turnings at once. We must change from an anthropocentric, androcentric view of the world to a biocentric, life-centered one. We must leave a dualistic model for a kinship one, seeing every creature linked to each other and to God in the dance of the universe. We must transform a culture that is spreading death to one that cherishes life. Simply put, all of us, women and men alike, need to fall in love with the earth as an inherently valuable, living community in which we participate, and be creatively faithful to it.

Warning against the delusion of the separated self, Albert Einstein emphasized, "Our task must be to free ourselves from this prison by widening our circle of compassion to embrace all living creatures and the whole of nature in its beauty."[49] Widening our circle of compassion would rejoin us to the cosmic covenant made after the biblical flood "between God and every living creature of all flesh that is on the earth," and whose sign is the rainbow (Gen 9:8-17). Such an embrace delivers us so to kinship with all creatures that we assume our responsibility as co-partners with the Creator Spirit in seeing to it that never again shall the earth be destroyed.

Coherent with feminist and other liberation spiritualities, being converted to the earth entails the mutually fertilizing elements of contemplation and prophecy.

CONTEMPLATION

Contemplation is a way of seeing that leads to communion. The fact that the world is simply there, in splendor and fragility, gives rise to wonder, leading to a religious sense of the loving power that quickens it. "The world is charged with the glory of God," exclaims poet Gerard Manley Hopkins,[50] echoing the ancient psalmist's praise that "The heavens are telling the glory of God" (Ps 19:1). In contemplation the human spirit learns to see the presence of the divine in nature, and so recognizes that the earth is a sacred place. For such a spirit the biblical bush still burns, and we take off our shoes.

Through contemplation the religious spirit grows in the realization of how deeply humanity is embedded in the earth. We begin to know this experientially, to feel in the depths of our being that we are part of the living cosmos. Consequently, we recover a capacity for subjective communion with the earth. We develop what Barbara McClintock, the Nobel prize-

63

winning biologist, calls "a deep feeling for the organism," which is a result of recognizing that we are all kin, related through ontological participation in the community of creation. Consequently, reciprocity rather than rape marks our approach. We reach out toward the earth not just with utilitarian intent, although that is appropriate within limits, but with non-violent appreciation for its own inherent value. The naturalist Louis Agassiz epitomizes this stance with his remark, "I spent the summer travelling. I got halfway across my backyard."[51]

To the contemplative spirit, the vivifying power of God flashes out from the simplest natural phenomenon, the smallest seed. "Speak to the earth and it will teach you," Job urges his ignorant but well-meaning friends (Job 12:7). "Look at the birds of the air" and "consider the lilies of the field," Jesus teaches his disciples, knowing that they will find there testimony to God's care (Mt 6:25-33). Earth, in a word, is a sacrament.[52] Pervaded and encircled by the Creator Spirit it effects by signifying the subtly active presence of the holy giver of life. Without the knowledge of contemplation, which is akin to prayer, prophetic action on behalf of the earth will in the long run fall short of the wisdom needed for its long-term cherishing.

PROPHECY

Prophecy is a way of speaking and acting in the face of powerful, oppressive interests that leads to repentance and renewal. On the one hand there is a dangerous edge to prophecy insofar as it denounces

64

wrongdoing and thus incurs the wrath of special interest groups that are benefiting. On the other hand prophecy's critical edge also cuts through the despair of those who are suffering, for it announces comfort and hope in the approach of God's renewing Spirit.

Shaped by contemplation of the sacredness of the living earth, the prophetic stance names new sins against God's gracious will: biocide, ecocide, geocide. Several billion years of creative toil and several million species of abounding life are now in the care of one late-coming species in which mind and morals have emerged. By what right do we even call ourselves *Homo sapiens* if we forget the wisdom of relatedness and ignore the immense creative investment that has gone into producing the earth? Words such as sacrilege, blasphemy, desecration are not too strong to label the violation.

Prophecy uses all the techniques of active, non-violent resistance to halt aggression against the vulnerable, be it ever so humble a species or ever so vast a system such as the ozone layer. Participating in the compassion of God, the prophetic community enters into solidarity with suffering creation and exercises responsibility for a new project of ecojustice.

In the process it takes one step further the sense of interconnection between the harmony of nature and social justice typical of the biblical prophets. Social injustice and ecological degradation are inextricably fused in theory and practice. In fact, structures of social domination are chief among the ways that exploitation of the earth is accomplished. Examples: the plantation system ruins biodiversity while it creates wealth for a few from the backbreaking labor of a class of poor people. Pressure on the rain forest from slash and burn subsistence farmers results from inequitable distribution of land to begin with. Appalachian land and water are despoiled by coal mining done for subsistence wages by communities that live amid the depleted hills and hollows, while owners' profits enable them to live miles away in beautiful natural surroundings. U.S. companies export work to factories across the Mexican border (*maquiladores*) that cheaply employ thousands of young, rural women to make high quality consumer goods while they live in unhealthy squalor in an environment spoiled with toxic waste. The environmental crisis is intertwined with a social system that allows a few to benefit by making a profit at the expense of the many in the form of low wages, bad working conditions, and poisonous side-effects.[53] Prophecy knows that remedying environmental degradation involves addressing dehumanizing poverty as part of a wholistic ethic based on interdependence rather than exploitation among human beings themselves and between human beings and the earth.

Liberation ethics in our age has come to grips with the plight of poor people, with their power as a locus of theological insight, and with the essential need to include their well-being in the vision and action of the gospel. In a similar way, being converted to the earth requires that we extend the justice model to embrace the whole earth. For westerners emerging from a heritage of dualism this is a new ethical horizon: that we extend moral consideration to species beyond our own, and moral standing to ecological systems as a whole. Such a move, however, is a logical outcome of conversion to the community of creation. Realization of our mutual kinship with the living earth leads us to encompass nature in the command to love one's neighbor as oneself. In the eloquent words of Brian Patrick:

> Who is our neighbor: the Samaritan? the outcast? the enemy? Yes, yes, of course. But it also the whale, the dolphin, and the rain forest. Our neighbor is the entire community of life, the entire universe. We must love it all as our self....[54]

A flourishing humanity on a thriving earth: such is the vision that shapes the prophetic course. Since it is the earth that is being destabilized by human practice, redressing the balance requires increased focus on the integrity of natural systems and the worth of non-human creatures. Accordingly, prophecy converted to the earth sees that making a preferential option for the poor includes other species and the ravaged natural world itself. Healing and redeeming this world, this intrinsically valuable matrix of our origin, growth, and fulfillment, has the character of a moral imperative. It urges us to act according to the criterion crafted by the naturalist Aldo Leopold: "A thing is right when it tends to preserve the integrity, stability, and beauty of the life community. It is wrong when it tends to do otherwise."[55] We are as large as our loves. The prophetic option for a biocentric ethic transforms us toward great-heartedness in its demand for universal compassion and cosmic praxis.

In this lecture I have sought a new vision of the Creator Spirit enfolding and unfolding a reconciled human community and a healed, living earth, to practical and critical effect. The precise point has been to overcome sexist disparagement of the female in the three basic relationships of human beings among each other, with the earth, and with God, and thereby to serve the future of life itself.

At the heart of physical reality we find a living communion, today under threat. Being converted to the earth in its hour of suffering places us in resonant cooperation with the deepest reality of creation, the Creator Spirit. When we work with people and movements committed to cherishing the earth and opposing its plunder, we are participating in the Spirit's own political economy of life. Instead of living as thoughtless or greedy exploiters we are empowered to become sisters and brothers, friends and lovers, gardeners and stewards, advocates and poets, priests and prophets, colleagues and fellow dancers, co-creators and children of the world that gives us life. Too much has already been lost. But the narrative memory of the dead, as always, has the capacity to bring about a living future if we cooperate with the compassionate power of the Creator Spirit. As a symbol of the solidarity between east and west on this issue, I close with the prayer uttered by Korean theologian Chung Hyun-Kyung in her Canberra address on peace, justice, and the integrity of creation. "Wild wind of the Holy Spirit blow, to us. Let us welcome her, letting ourselves go in her wild rhythm of life. Come, Holy Spirit, renew the whole creation. Amen!"[56]

APPENDIX [57]

Religious Environmental Groups

The Center for Reflection on the Second Law, 8420 Camellia Dr., Raleigh, NC 27613.

Center of Concern, 3700 13th St. NE, Washington, DC 20017.

Eco-Justice Project Network, Center for Religion, Ethics and Social Policy, Anabel Taylor Hall, Cornell University, Ithaca, NY 14853.

Institute in Culture and Creation Spirituality, Holy Names College, 3500 Mountain Blvd., Oakland, CA 94619.

Interfaith Center on Corporate Responsibility, 475 Riverside Drive, Rm. 566, New York, NY 10115.

Interfaith Coalition on Energy, P.O. Box 26577, Philadelphia, PA 19141.

Justice, Peace, and Integrity of Creation, World Council of Churches, P.O. Box 2100, CH-1211, Geneva 2, Switzerland.

The Land Stewardship Council of North Carolina, Rte. 4, Box 426, Pittsboro, NC 27312.

Land Stewardship Project, 14758 Ostlund Trail North, Marine, MN 55047.

The National Catholic Rural Life Conference, 4625 Beaver Ave., Des Moines, IA 50310.

The North American Conference on Christianity and
    Ecology, P.O. Box 14305, San Francisco, CA
    94114.
Riverdale Center of Religious Research, 5801 Palisade
    Ave., Riverdale, NY 10471.

General Environmental Organizations

Council on Economic Priorities, 30 Irving Place, New
    York, NY 10022.
Environmental Action Foundation, 1525 New
    Hampshire Ave. NW, Washington, DC 20036.
Environmental Protection Agency, Public Information
    Center, 401 M St. SW, Washington, DC 20460.
Friends of the Earth, 218 D St. SE, Washington, DC
    20003.
Global Tomorrow Coalition, 1325 G St. NW,
    Washington, DC 20005.
Greenpeace USA, 1426 U St. NW, Washington, DC
    20036.
Inform, 381 Park Ave. South, New York, NY 10060.
Izaac Walton Club, 1701 N. Ft. Myer Drive #1100,
    Arlington, VA 22209.
The Nature Conservancy, 1815 N. Lynn St., Arlington,
    VA 22209.
Rocky Mountain Institute, 1739 Snowmass Creek Rd.,
    Snowmass, CO 81654.
Seventh Generation, 126 Intervale Rd., Burlington, VT
    05401.
Sierra Club, 730 Polk St., San Francisco, CA 94109.
Union of Concerned Scientists, 26 Church St.,
    Cambridge, MA 02238.

United Nations Environmental Programme, DC2-0803
United Nations, New York, NY 10017.

World Resources Institute, 1709 New York Ave. NW,
Washington, DC 20006.

Worldwatch Institute, 1776 Massachusetts Ave. NW,
Washington, DC 20036.

World Wildlife Fund, 1250 24th St. NW, Washington,
DC 20037.

NOTES

1. My thanks to Patricia Bauman and the Bauman Foundation for arranging the viewing of "Blue Planet"; also to Kevin Irwin for orchestrating the conference on "Preserving the Creation: Environmental Theology and Ethics" at Georgetown University, 1992. The ideas in this lecture germinated in that setting.

2. Cited in Michael Dowd, *Earthspirit: A Handbook for Nurturing an Ecological Christianity* (Mystic, CT: Twenty-Third Pub., 1991) 54.

3. Catherine Keller, "Women Against Wasting the World: Notes on Eschatology and Ecology," in *Reweaving the World: The Emergence of Ecofeminism,* ed. Irene Diamond and Gloria Feman Orenstein (San Francisco: Sierra Club Books, 1990) 249.

4. For a careful analysis of the dimensions of the ecological crisis see James Nash, *Loving Nature: Ecological Integrity and Christian Responsibility* (Nashville: Abingdon Press, 1991), espec. chaps. 1 and 2.

5. Among the pioneers in religious thinking are Thomas Berry, *The Dream of the Earth* (San Francisco: Sierra Club Books, 1988); Matthew Fox, *The Coming of the Cosmic Christ* (San Francisco: Harper & Row, 1988); Douglas Hall, *Imaging God: Dominion as Stewardship* (Grand Rapids:

Eerdmans, 1986); Sallie McFague, *Models of God: Theology for an Ecological, Nuclear Age* (Philadelphia: Fortress, 1987); and Jürgen Moltmann, *God in Creation: A New Theology of Creation and the Spirit of God* (San Francisco: Harper & Row, 1985).

6. In addition to Diamond and Orenstein, *Reweaving the World,* which has an extended bibliography, see Judith Plante, ed., *Healing the Wounds: The Promise of Ecofeminism* (Philadelphia: Fortress, 1984); and Lois Daly, "Ecofeminism, Reverence for Life, and Feminist Theological Ethics," in *Liberating Life: Contemporary Approaches to Ecological Theology,* Charles Birch, William Eakin, and Jay McDaniel, eds. (Maryknoll, NY: Orbis, 1990) 88-108. Classic statements of the women-earth connection are Rosemary Radford Ruether, *New Woman, New Earth* (San Francisco: Harper & Row, 1975); and Susan Griffin, *Woman and Nature: The Roaring Inside Her* (San Francisco: Harper & Row, 1978).

7. Rosemary Radford Ruether, *To Change the World: Christology and Cultural Criticism* (NY: Crossroad, 1981) 60. See the essays on the construction of gender in Anne Carr and Elisabeth Schüssler Fiorenza, eds., *The Special Nature of Women?* (Philadelphia: Trinity Press International, 1991), *Concilium* 1991/6.

8. These developments are succinctly explored by J. Baird Callicott, "The Metaphysical Implications of Ecology," in *Nature in Asian Traditions of Thought,* Callicott and Roger Ames, eds. (Albany: SUNY Press, 1989) 51-64; and Margaret Farley, "Feminist Theology and Bioethics," in *Women's Consciousness, Women's Conscience,* Barbara Hilkert Andolsen, Christine Gudorf, & Mary Pellauer, eds. (Minneapolis: Winston Press, 1985) 285-305.

9. Cited in Carolyn Merchant, *The Death of Nature: Women,*

Ecology, and the Scientific Revolution (San Francisco: Harper & Row, 1980) 168.

10. Cited in ibid. 170.

11. Sherry Ortner, "Is Female to Male as Nature Is to Culture?" in *Women, Culture, and Society*, Michelle Zimbalist Rosaldo and Louise Lamphere, eds. (Stanford: Stanford University Press, 1974) 67-87.

12. Catherine Keller, "Feminism and the Ethic of Inseparability," in *Weaving the Visions: New Patterns in Feminist Spirituality*, Judith Plaskow and Carol Christ, eds. (San Francisco: Harper & Row, 1989) 256-65; see Michael Zimmerman, "Deep Ecology and Ecofeminism: The Emerging Dialogue," in Diamond and Orenstein, *Reweaving the World,* 138-54.

13. Ruether, *New Woman, New Earth,* 11.

14. Heribert Mühlen, "The Person of the Holy Spirit," *The Holy Spirit and Power,* ed. Kilian McDonnell (Garden City, NY: Doubleday, 1975) 12.

15. For fuller treatment of this point see Elizabeth Johnson, *SHE WHO IS: The Mystery of God in Feminist Theological Discourse* (NY: Crossroad, 1992) 124-49.

16. Margaret Farley, "Feminist Ethics," *Westminster Dictionary of Christian Ethics,* James Childress and John Macquarrie, eds. (Philadelphia: Westminster, 1986) 230. For extended discussion see Anne Carr, *Transforming Grace: Christian Tradition and Women's Experience* (San Francisco: Harper & Row, 1988); and Rosemary Radford Ruether, *Sexism and God-Talk: Toward a Feminist Theology* (Boston: Beacon, 1983).

17. Bell Hooks, *Feminist Theory: From Margin to Center* (Boston: South End Press, 1984) ix. Rebecca Chopp, *The Power to Speak: Feminism, Language, God* (NY: Crossroad, 1989) 15-18 and 115-124 offer a fine analysis of marginality.

18. Paula Cooey, Sharon Farmer, & Mary Ellen Ross, eds., *Embodied Love: Sensuality and Relationship as Feminist Values* (San Francisco: Harper & Row, 1987); and Plaskow & Christ, *Weaving the Visions*, Part 3.

19. Nancy Chodorow, *The Reproduction of Mothering* (Berkeley: University of California Press, 1978); and Catherine Keller, *From a Broken Web: Separation, Sexism and Self* (Boston: Beacon, 1986). Margaret Farley closely relates this factor to the development of ethical norms: "New Patterns of Relationship: Beginnings of a Moral Revolution," *Theological Studies* 36 (1975) 627-46.

20. Ruether, *To Change the World*, 67; the example of the trees is also taken from her. This pattern of relationship is beautifully described in Katherine Zappone, *The Hope for Wholeness: A Spirituality for Feminists* (Mystic, CT: Twenty-Third Pub., 1991).

21. McFague, *Models of God*, 7-8.

22. Starhawk, *Truth or Dare* (San Francisco: Harper & Row, 1987) 1. I follow the story of creation as told by William Pollard, "The Uniqueness of the Earth," in *Earth Might Be Fair: Reflections on Ethics, Religion, and Ecology*, Ian Barbour, ed. (Englewood Cliffs, NJ: Prentice-Hall, 1972) 82-99. See also Carl Sagan, *Cosmos* (NY: Ballantine, 1980); and Denis Edwards, *Jesus and the Cosmos* (NY: Paulist, 1991), chap. 2.

23. Arthur Peacocke, "Theology and Science Today," in *Cosmos as Creation*, Ted Peters, ed. (Nashville: Abingdon,

1989) 32.

24. Sean McDonagh, *To Care for the Earth* (Santa Fe: Bear, 1986) 118-19. For theological interpretation see John Haught, *The Cosmic Adventure* (NY: Paulist, 1984).

25. See lucid discussion in David Toolan, *Nature Is a Heraclitean Fire* (St. Louis: Seminar on Jesuit Spirituality, 1991) 19-32.

26. Teilhard de Chardin, cited in Dowd, *Earthspirit,* 17. Teilhard was a pioneer of this vision: *The Divine Milieu* (NY: Harper, 1960).

27. Cited in Ruth Lechte, "Partnership for Ecological Wellbeing," *The Ecumenical Review* 42 (April 1990) 158.

28. Thomas Aquinas, *Summa Theologiae* I, q. 47, a.1.

29. Cited by Sallie McFague, "Imaging a Theology of Nature: The World as God's Body," in Birch, *Liberating Life,* 225.

30. These images are suggested by Tertullian, *Adversus Praxeas* 8. See Brian Gaybba, *The Spirit of Love* (London: Chapman, 1987) for a history of the doctrine of the Spirit.

31. Metaphors from the hymn "Veni Sancte Spiritus," Sequence for the feast of Pentecost. See also Karl Rahner, "The Spirit That Is Over All Life," *Theological Investigations,* Vol. 7 (NY: Herder & Herder, 1971) 193-201; and José Comblin, *The Holy Spirit and Liberation* (Maryknoll, NY: Orbis, 1989).

32. The biblical view is delineated by Eduard Schweizer, *The Holy Spirit* (Philadelphia: Fortress, 1980); natural images

described in Paul Newman, *A Spirit Christology* (Lanham, MD: University Press of America, 1987) 69-74.

33. Ann Belford Ulanov, *The Feminine: In Jungian Psychology and in Christian Theology* (Evanston: Northwestern University Press, 1971) 325.

34. Meinrad Craighead, *The Mother's Songs: Images of God the Mother* (NY: Paulist, 1986) 65.

35. Ibid.

36. Cyril of Jerusalem *Catechetical Lectures* 17.13, in *The Holy Spirit,* J. Patout Burns and Gerald Fagin, eds. (Wilmington, DE: Glazier, 1984) 34-35.

37. From *Hildegard of Bingen: Mystical Writings,* Fiona Bowie & Oliver Davies, eds. (NY: Crossroad, 1990) 91-93.

38. Irenaeus, *Adversus Haereses* Book 3, chap. 17.2; in Burns and Fagin, 34-35.

39. Cyril of Jerusalem, *Catechetical Lectures,* 16.12, in Burns and Fagin, 94.

40. Hildegaard of Bingen, *Scivias,* trans. Mother Columba Hart and Jane Bishop (NY: Paulist, 1990) 190 and passim. Here I render only the metaphors and not the full Hart/Bishop translation, which articulates the Spirit as "it."

41. Basil of Caesarea, *On the Holy Spirit*, chap. 19.49, in Burns and Fagin, 126.

42. See Johnson, *SHE WHO IS*, 86-100.

43. Genesis *Rabbah* 86:6, cited in Dale Moody, "Shekinah,"

Interpreter's Dictionary of the Bible (Nashville: Abingdon, 1962) 4:317-19.

44. *Bar. Meg.* 29a, cited in Moody, ibid.

45. Sandra Schneiders, *Women and the Word* (NY: Paulist, 1986) 38.

46. Cited in Robert Murray, "Holy Spirit as Mother," in *Symbols of Church and Kingdom* (London: Cambridge University, 1975) 315.

47. Cited in E. Pataq-Siman, *L'Expérience de l'Esprit d'après la tradition syrienne d'Antioche* (Théologie historique 15, Paris: 1971) 155.

48. Arthur Peacocke, critically discussed in Ian Barbour, *Religion in an Age of Science* (San Francisco: Harper & Row, 1990) 177-78.

49. Cited in Dowd, *Earthspirit*, 81.

50. Gerard Manley Hopkins, "God's Grandeur," *A Hopkins Reader*, John Pick, ed. (Garden City, NY: Doubleday, 1966) 47-48.

51. Cited in Holms Rolston, *Philosophy Gone Wild: Essays in Environmental Ethics* (Buffalo, NY: Prometheus, 1986) 241.

52. Michael Himes and Kenneth Himes, "The Sacrament of Creation: Toward an Environmental Theology," *Commonweal* 117 (Jan. 26, 1990) 42-49.

53. See discussion in Nash, *Loving Nature*; and Ruether, *Sexism and God-Talk,* Postscript.

54. Cited in Dowd, *Earthspirit*, 40.

55. Cited in Dowd, *Earthspirit*, 41. See Aldo Leopold, *A Sand County Almanac* (NY: Oxford University Press, 1949). There is potential for developing this view within Catholic social teaching; see *Renewing the Earth: An Invitation to Reflection and Action on Environment in Light of Catholic Social Teaching* (Washington DC: United States Catholic Conference, Nov. 14, 1991).

56. Chung Hyun-Kyung, address to the World Council of Churches, Canberra Assembly, 1991. See Mary Evelyn Tucker, "Expanding Contexts, Breaking Boundaries: the Challenge of Chung Hyun-Kyung," *Cross Currents* 42 (1992) 236-43; and Michael Putney, "Come Holy Spirit, Renew the Whole Creation: Seventh Assembly of the World Council of Churches," *Theological Studies* 52 (1991) 607-35.

57. Adapted from Toolan, *Nature Is a Heraclitean Fire*, 45-46.

The Madeleva Lecture in Spirituality

This series, sponsored by the Center for Spirituality, Saint Mary's College, Notre Dame, Indiana, honors annually the woman who as president of the college inaugurated its pioneering graduate program in theology, Sister M. Madeleva, C.S.C.

1985
Monika K. Hellwig
Christian Women in a Troubled World

1986
Sandra M. Schneiders
Women and the Word

1987
Mary Collins
Women at Prayer

1988
Maria Harris
Women and Teaching

1989
Elizabeth Dreyer
Passionate Women: Two Medieval Mystics

1990
Joan Chittister
Job's Daughters

1991
Dolores R. Leckey
Women and Creativity

1992
Lisa Sowle Cahill
Women and Sexuality

1993
Elizabeth A. Johnson
Women, Earth and Creator Spirit

1994
Gail Porter Mandell
Madeleva: One Woman's Life

1995
Diana L. Hayes
Hagar's Daughters

1996
Jeanette Rodriguez
Stories We Live
Cuentos Que Vivimos

1997
Mary C. Boys
Jewish-Christian Dialogue
One Woman's Experience

1998
Kathleen Norris
The Quotidian Mysteries
Laundry, Liturgy and "Women's Work"